OPERATING IN ABUNDANCE

GET READY TO OPEN THE DOORWAY TO DIVINE MYSTERY THROUGH **THE 23RD PSALM**

DR. ADONIJAH OGBONNAYA

אתה

OPERATING IN ABUNDANCE
Adonijah O. Ogbonnaya, Ph. D.

Aactev8 International1020 Victoria Ave. Venice, CA 90291

www.aactev8.com

Published by Seraph Creative 2020
ISBN: 978-1-922428-04-2

Edited by Kathy Strecker

Library of Congress data

Alchemy, prayer, provisions, personal growth, spirituality. The Lord's Prayer, Will, will of man, will of God, Kingdom of God, heaven, forgiveness, temptation, spiritual power, transformation, Bible study.

Scripture quotations from the New American Standard Bible, unless otherwise stated.

ESV, NIV, NKJV, KJV

Cover art by Feline Graphics

Typesetting, Illustration & Layout by Feline
www.felinegraphics.com

אתה

CONTENTS

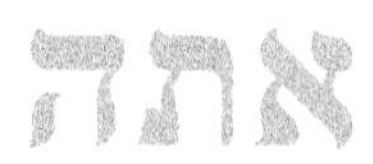

FOREWORD

When I first preached these messages at our local church in Venice, God promised me that He would show people the heart of abundance as I was preaching, and that our community, and my global family would move into a greater level of abundance.

Let me say, this book is not just about money, or finances, or even just about business, this book is written to help you become a person of generosity. As I complete this book, I stand in awe of God's divine plan, in the midst of the Covid-19 pandemic when the earth moved to a place of fear and lack.

As I release this revelation, I trust that God will move in your life, to change the operating system of your life, this book enables the believer to walk on the path of abundance, being a person of wealth, in every area of life.

I used the template of Psalm 23, a well-known scripture in the eyes of many, however allow me to illuminate your path again, as God has shone His divine light when revealing the hidden mysteries of this scripture to me.

I believe this book will provide you with keys to freedom, keys that will be with you for the rest of your life, as David, the friend of God, learned the ways of God, so you can walk in those same paths, into a place where the living water of God never runs out in every area of your life.

We serve a God who has given to us abundantly, His only Son, Jesus Christ, not just the Saviour of the world, but a gift from a Father to His children, saying to humanity, I value you more than gold, and silver, I value you more than my creation, I can only show you my love by sending my Son, to show you the very heart of generosity.

I pray that God will bless you, as you learn the ways of righteousness in this book, may the Spirit of Wisdom impart to you, the wisdom to walk in ways that will bless your generations, and change the very frequency of your life, to joy, hope and a beautiful wonder and awe of the provision of God.

May God bless you and keep you.

Shalom
Dr Adonijah O. Ogbonnaya

אתה

HOW TO READ THIS BOOK

Psalm 23 is probably one of the most famous and well-loved bible passages of all time. To be sure, it's the psalm we first turn to as we cry out to our Father in times of need. Though this psalm is constantly at our fingertips, Dr. Ogbonnaya tells us that Psalm 23 contains significant truths and mysteries that we have not yet grasped nor appropriated into the way we relate to God and operate within His provision for us.

Operating in Abundance takes us on a journey to unlock the mysteries of Psalm 23 and enter a realm of discovery of the true essence of our Father's heart. Dr. Ogbonnaya meanders the pathways that David himself traveled to help us encounter the nature of God and how far He goes to pursue us with His relentless love. Along the way, Dr. Ogbonnaya stops to unravel hidden levels of meaning and expounds on the significance of keywords and phrases, explaining how the Hebrew letters and the gematria enrich and support the deeper truths of God's goodness and mercy.

Come on this journey, armed with prayer and a spirit ready to demolish old paradigms and ways of thinking. Get ready to discover even more about our Father's goodness and tap into the endless possibilities of His eternal provision. There is a chart of the Aleph Bet at the end of the book to support you as Dr. Ogbonnaya breaks down certain words and phrases into their component parts in the Hebrew.

Get ready to open the door to His divine mysteries!

אתה

Psalm 23

King James Version (NASBKJV)

The Lord, is My Shepherd.

A Psalm of David.

1The LORD *is* my shepherd; I shall not want.

2He maketh me to lie down in green pastures:
he leadeth me beside the still waters.

3He restoreth my soul: he leadeth me in the
paths of righteousness for his name's sake.

4Yea, though I walk through the valley of the shadow of death,
I will fear no evil: for thou *art* with me;
thy rod and thy staff they comfort me.

5Thou preparest a table before me in the presence of mine enemies:
thou anointest my head with oil; my cup runneth over.

6Surely goodness and mercy shall follow me all the days of my life:
and I will dwell in the house of the LORD for ever.

אתה

Chapter 1

OUR EVER-PRESENT PROVIDER

In this day and age, we need to reconsider our perspective on provision.

All wars and all struggles, from my point of view, are fought because human beings have been trained for millennia to believe that there is not enough, and it comes from the place of lack. I began to look at some of the great wars that have been fought in the world and a majority have been about economics. A lot of our fears and anxieties derive from not having enough. Even quarrels within the family often have to do with provision or the lack thereof. We may have everything, yet we still think we don't have enough. There is something in our psyche that has bought into the idea that there is never enough. We think if we don't see it, it is not there. *In other words, our tendency to spiritualize and materialize lack ends up making us not understand anything beyond what we can see.* We've also been taught that everything we have, everything that's ever happened to us, *we* have worked for. That's a lie. We are guided by a lot of false assumptions around our understanding of provision.

Why would Israel ask for another god? There is nothing they needed in the wilderness that God didn't provide. Even God Himself was not enough for them. They needed a god they could see, touch, and play with, which means they needed a god less than themselves. They didn't have to do anything for God to bring them out of Egypt—He provided everything. They didn't create the lamb whose blood they used on the door post. They didn't even know what happened that night because an angel went to make the Egyptians release them. Everything that happened to them was a miracle of divine providence. God was fully present, but even the presence of God was not enough because they had been trained to believe that there is never enough.

If you understand the miracle of the Red Sea from the Jewish perspective, you will see what God did. The bible says that Israel went into the sea and the sea was a wall on each side. So in other words they had the sea above them and on the sides. They walked through a tunnel, which formed the letter "Heh" because the letter is a doorway to another dimension. The bible also says,

> The angel of God, who had been going before the camp of Israel, moved and went behind them; and the pillar of cloud moved from before them and stood behind them. So it came between the camp of Egypt and the camp of Israel; and there was the cloud along with the darkness, yet it gave light at night. Thus the one did not come near the other all night. (Exodus 14:19-20 NASB)

Regarding this passage, many of the Jewish fathers said by the combination of the Hebrew letters and the combination of the name of God, Moses was able to create an angelic structure to stand the water up and in between them and the Egyptians. God is letting Israel know that they are in an eternal, infinite position. There is *nothing* that God cannot become for them.

> You could be suffering the same experience with another human being and, depending on your perspective, you will survive and they won't

When Israel crossed to the other side, the scriptures say that God made the wheels of the Egyptians heavy, Remember that the scripture also says that there was darkness between this side and the other side and that the Egyptians could not cross to the other side, meaning Israel was in a different dimension. Israel understood they could go to another dimension since they went into the water. This means that you can be in the same tunnel as another person and, while their wheels are getting heavy, you move through easily. You could be suffering the same experience with another human being and, depending on your perspective, you will survive, and they won't. When Israel came out of the tunnel, they experienced provision at every turn. God didn't change the process, He merely took the same angelic structure that existed in the water, and placed it around them as seen in the darkness, the pillar of fire by night, and the pillar of cloud by day. It is the same process protecting them from whatever it is they are afraid of that might come against them. When they cry out, that same presence releases provision--whether it is food or shelter, it was there. David said, "They ate the food of angels." Jesus said,

"I am that bread in the wilderness." God wanted Israel to understand that they were slaves, a people who operate out of a position of lack, but they didn't have to worry about provision.

If you start from lack, everyone around you is going to be imperfect. Lack is not simply about food, but everything that sustains your life. There is nothing anybody can do for you that will satisfy you. This principle was what God was communicating with Israel if you understand that there is enough, you can be satisfied, and if you are satisfied, you can love your brothers and sisters. You don't have to go to war against your Spouse. Your idea of lack is what has gotten you into trouble. By not being satisfied in what you have around you, you are constantly searching for something that isn't there, and by doing so you are walking around in emptiness. As a result, you don't think you are enough because your world is informed by a fundamental sense of lack. By living out a fundamental sense of lack, you create idols that are less than you to become your guardian.

Whenever I think there is not enough, I walk in fear and anxiety which forces me to think of people as things. Your goal is not to be an angel, but a human being. When you don't take the time to examine yourself, you cease to be a human being because you think you are something that you're not. Why do you behave to others the way you do? By examining yourself, you don't ask for somebody else to repent. The job is not to make others repent but rather to rectify ourselves and to keep ourselves in a position that allows us to see the way God is and how He relates to us. God does not relate to us in partiality and out of lack.

> If you operate from a place of lack, you can never be at rest. The answer to your restlessness could be to change the perspective about God's capacity to provide for you.

The Shepherd always smells like the sheep. He is always in the midst of the sheep whether they are sick or healthy. The reason we operate in a consciousness of lack is because we fail to realize that God is present. God is the carrier of all provision in the universe, and it is from His innermost being that the universe comes into existence, worlds are continuously being created, and you and I were created. If all that is true, then it stands to reason that we are carriers of this same divine provision! Everything that is inside of God, we have access to because the breath of God drives the being of God into our whole being. When God breathes, He gives us life. When we breathe, we receive from God. The interconnection of breath means that the same fullness in the Father comes into you and me. We are not even speaking of the Upper soul, we are referring to the lower soul because your breath that gave you nefesh is your lower soul and even the animals have nefesh. When you breathe, you are not just engaging in a physical function, but you are reminding God of the fullness of His being that is supposed to come to you. That is why the writer of Ecclesiastes says, "When there is breath, there is hope."

"The Lord is my shepherd; I shall not want."

Where does want come from? From the inner sense of lack. "I shall not want/lack/be without/go without." The word in Hebrew from "want" is "Achsar" which means "I shall never have an empty hand." In your hands are written the scrolls of destiny. This is why palm readers read your hand. All the ancients believe there is a scroll written on your hand. The bible says in Psalm 91:12 that the angels shall bear you up in their hands. No one can undo the record of God's intent inscribed upon the palm of your hand. "I Shall" is used as an imperative, an assurance, because the presence of Yahweh ensures that my hands are always full with the record and outflowing of His divine intent which the bible says is His good will.

<u>If you operate from a place of lack, you can never be at rest.</u> The answer to your restlessness could be to change the perspective about God's capacity to provide for you.

"He leadeth me beside still waters."

The only place where still waters exist is in the throne room. John says the sea was like glass, so still that there was not even a ripple in it. How did David know that there are still waters? Because he has been there according to 2 Samuel 23 where it says, "David, the son of Jesse, the man who was taken up into heaven."

<u>What God is doing is making sure you don't have an excuse for walking in lack</u>. You claim the devil was your problem, so God conquered the devil at the cross. You said it was your sin that was the problem, so God gave His blood to wash away your sin. You said that it was darkness, so God made you light. You said you have no friends, so God became your friend and surrounded you with angels. You operate in lack when you forget the truth that Yahweh is our ever-present Provider and that we receive all things from Him.

אתה

אתה

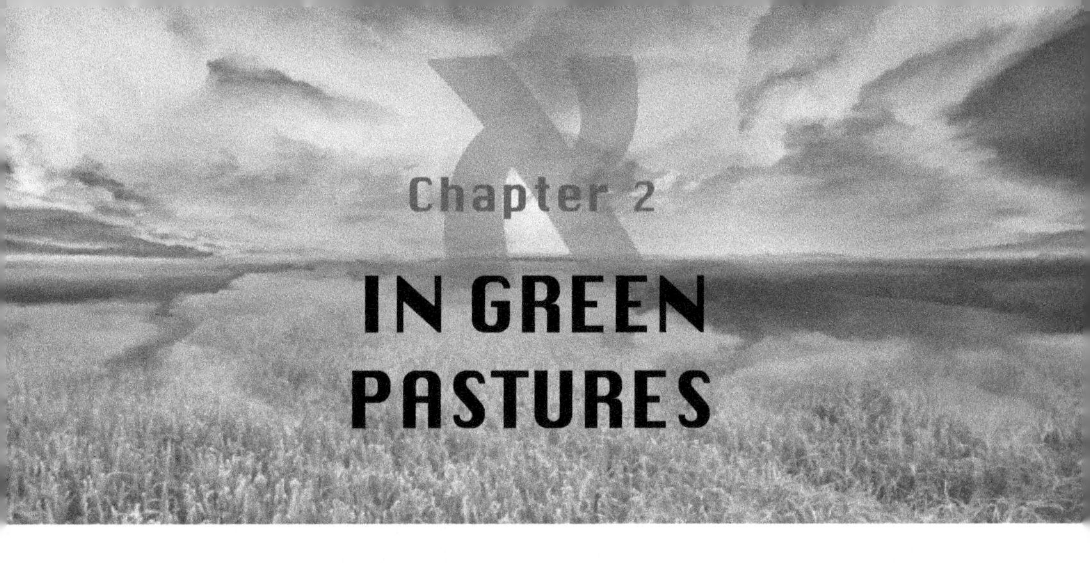

Chapter 2

IN GREEN PASTURES

How do we move away from the mind of lack to the mind of plenty.

We have been trained to operate from a position of lack. All the walls in the world are based on the idea of scarcity or anxiety. All anxieties are based on an underlying sense of scarcity. If you deal with the mental structure of scarcity, you open up a human being to the flow of abundance. Politics is based on the idea of scarcity. Economics is based on the idea of scarcity that there's limited resources on earth and that we need to make sure people don't get too much. We consistently operate on the basis of scarcity and it affects everything we do. Yet David pens this passage of scripture: "The Lord is my shepherd I shall not want." Like David, you need to be in a place where your life is without a sense of lack--not that there is *no* lack, but there's not a *sense* of lack. The psalm doesn't say that there's no lack; it says, "I shall not want." By uttering these words, David actually places abundance in the internal structure of himself.

The word used for "shepherd" in Psalm 23 is Ra'ah (רָאָה). I love the idea of Ra'ah because it means more than just a shepherd who takes care of his sheep. Ra'ah could mean, "The Lord is my way of seeing." The Lord is my way of seeing because the Hebrew word Jireh (יִרְאֶה) also means to see, not really provision. So when you said Jehovah Yireh, you're not really saying the Lord is my provider because that's not what it actually means. What you are saying is that the Lord sees and is therefore my way of seeing. Why is this important? Remember how God created the world—He spoke, right? And then He saw your life is not only determined by what you say, it is also determined by how you see. "The Lord is my way of seeing; I shall not want." So my way of seeing as God sees opens my being to the overflow of abundance because every human being carries within their internal structure the full record of divine provision until the human being is trained to see from the perspective of scarcity.

So how do you see? David proceeds to say this:

"He makes me lie down in green pastures."

> Rest is not sleep; rest is an uncommon calmness and inner tranquility when nothing moves you within

In the dwelling place of grassy fields, He makes me lie down or makes me to rest. When a verse begins like that, it tells you some of the principles and technology for harnessing and releasing the abundance in ourselves. For example, if scarcity causes anxiety and restlessness, then a sense of abundance causes rest. Maybe the reason you're all anxious is that your mind is focused on what you don't have and what you think you may never have. Or maybe you think everybody else is getting it, but it's going to run out before you get there. If that is the case, you're operating in the car salesman model—get yours before it's all gone! It's the last sale of the year! You know every advertisement is letting us know this stuff is going to run out. If we don't rush, if we don't do this, if we don't do that, then it's going to just run out, and then we're going to be left out. The next year, we get the same advertisements, and we respond the same way.

In the house of the grassy meadows, He makes me to rest.

This principle of rest is always the technology for releasing the abundance or the scroll of abundance of divinity that was in God's mind and intent before He created you. A lot of us think rest is sleep. Rest is not sleep; rest is an uncommon calmness and inner tranquility when nothing moves you within. Rest is being in the center of the storm where the wave doesn't exist even though it's all around you. That is what happens if you know yourself and you have a way of seeing that focuses on the right place. Do you know you can look on something terrible and it will either cause you anxiety or you can still have peace depending on how you look at it? Be careful how you look!

Remember God starts talking about rest from Genesis. I will give you rest, I will give you rest, I will give you rest, I will give you rest, I will give you the rest. Rest is not a cessation from work. Rest is not a cessation from activity. It is an inner peace. In Africa, we say a great dancer is someone who moves and yet is still. In Europe, you call it grace. So if the dancer has grace, she makes the dance look easy. Find that center and stay there no matter what. This centering is not you sitting at home watching television, eating burritos and drinking coca-cola. That is not rest - that's laziness. Good warriors are always at rest in themselves.

So resting in the depth of your being is not laziness. Too many believers think resting is stopping everything. Do you know God is at rest. Jesus said my Father works until now and I work also and yet the Bible says God rested. It is a mystery of its own—God, who works and is at rest, is who God is. The idea of rest is probably one of the greatest keys for unlocking the depth of what is inside of you, that sense of "be still and be anxious for nothing." One of the ways you know that you have rest is if you believe something absolutely and it doesn't matter what happens around you. Faith is an expression of rest, not a mental agitation which is what many of us have turned faith into. "You got to believe!" Actually, faith that works from rest is more powerful than faith that works from business. Do you notice what God said about Israel? He said, "I'm not bringing them into my rest because they do not believe." So faith creates rest, but rest gives birth to faith because if you don't believe, you will not be at peace and if you're not at peace, you won't believe. It is the mystery of the chicken and the egg.

Next, David says, "He leads me beside still waters." Again, the English translation is not really helpful because the word that is used for "beside" is the word **'al (עַל)**. This word means "upon" or "hover over," not by the side of the water. I want you to understand the difference now so **'al** means He leads me upon the waters, upon still waters. It changes our perspective, doesn't it? Now instead of you walking by the river, you are actually in the center of the river and you are on the river, you are *upon* or *hovering over* the river. Water is a symbol of abundance. The sea has more creatures than the land does; it is the source of abundance. In fact, one of the blessings that Jacob gave to one of his sons was "the abundance of the sea shall come to you." David is not actually talking about the sea on earth because the sea on earth is not still. He is talking about the sea in heaven because it's

> The idea of rest is probably one of the greatest keys for unlocking the depth of what is inside of you, that sense of "be still and be anxious for nothing."

the only place where there is a sea that produces without agitation. In Revelation 15:2, it says, "I saw a sea and it was as quiet or as smooth as glass." It's not the sea of glass—it looks like glass. The point is it is a sea that is completely still and no matter what you do to it, it has no ripple in it. There is no ripple in it because it is not a sea in time. There is no time ripple because it's in the place of eternity. Nothing moves it which means it is a sea of changelessness. If you're operating on that sea and God places you there, seasons don't matter to you because you are living at the very source of life. Time and changes and vicissitudes do not matter. Whether you are young, old, black, gray, or have black, red, or blue hair, you being on the sea means you're standing from the place where God releases abundance upon the earth. You are not under the sea; you are on top of the sea. It is a place of dominion and rulership. Remember rest is a place of calm that produces abundance without agitation.

Wealth is not from outside; it is from inside!

The story of France is a good place to talk a little bit. France is one of the first nations to start giving people weekends off. During that time, everyone said that France is going to die economically. However, they discovered very quickly that the more they give their people a place to rest, the more their productivity went up. We now know that when somebody rests, they come back to work and have more energy, so now it's a law in the nation. You can't make somebody work for more than three hours straight without a break especially if it's a manual work. Even the organizational psychologists know that these things are necessary.

It's an inbuilt law in nature that when you give something rest, it renews itself. So rest! When you operate in rest, you activate the abundance in you and doing this gives you the next place where David says, "He restores my soul" Something happens in you that causes rejuvenation and in rejuvenation you're producing something new every time. It gives you access to your unconscious. Until you are at rest, your unconscious is unaccessible to you. You're operating from your sub-conscious which is where you push all of your mess. Your unconscious is where all the records of your soul that came with you from heaven have been pushed because of how society has trained you and you can access it because everything you're doing is based on your pain and your bad experiences. You're operating from the perspective of mess but when you rest, you reach into a divine consciousness that you cannot reach when you are so busy worrying about stuff.

You are the abundance! Let me talk about this in terms of capitalism

In reality, we are not paid because of the person we work for. You are paid because of what you carry. Think about it this way. You take what is inside of you, you give it to somebody, and the person gives you cash. Wealth is not from outside; it is from inside! The only way wealth can truly be accessed is by coming to rest. That's why Jesus says, "Come unto me all ye that labor and are heavy laden and I will give you rest." Then the Bible proceeds to tell you to labor to enter into his rest. Your focus should be to come to a place of rest. Like Bobby McFerrin says, "Don't worry! Be happy!"

אתה

Chapter 3

PATHS OF RIGHTEOUSNESS

In the next phrase, David says, "He guides me in paths of righteousness for His name's sake."

Our problem, like I told you before, is that we've been brought up with a concept of scarcity., We all were brought up with the idea that things are running out and that's a fundamental problem for us which is why we cannot operate in the fullness of the increase of the Father. It's such a strong thing in us that we even think God does not have enough. You may say you don't think like that but I have talked to believers who say things like there are other people that God needs to take care of and I don't want to disturb God or I don't want to trouble God. Actually I counsel people who say stuff like that and so part of this problem is that in our society and from the time we were born, it was ingrained in us that the world is living in scarcity. We kill each other because we think there's not enough. We get offended even over job positions because we think there's only a few positions to fill.

When you see two people quarreling over some things that we know God provides in abundance, just recognize that we are not thinking rationally according to God's truth. It's the way we operate. However, I want to give you an encouragement that you were brought into this world with a full abundance of the supply of the Father. God did not actually take away the supply from Adam; He just said that man is going to sweat to manifest it. You are going to sweat to manifest it. He never said there's not going to be abundance. He said from now on you're going to sweat to access it. So you begin with an affirmation of the fact that you came from abundance and you operate in abundance and you live in abundance and you walk towards the manifestation of abundance. It's in you! This is not a prosperity message. I have a problem with that type of message, but I don't want you to think that God is a God of lack or that God is a God of scarcity. Does God run out when it comes your turn? If you really believe that, then your life and the way you perceive things will be different from how you behave. David says "The Lord is my shepherd; I shall not want." I like the way the word "want" is translated in the text because want has to do with a constant perception that I need something that has not been supplied.

If God is the shepherd, it is the responsibility of the shepherd to take the sheep to the place of supply. There are things you're worried about that are not your responsibility. What is the responsibility of the sheep? To eat when they get to the pasture. Do you find a sheep trying to plant grass? Your supply is so full that the only reason you're not having it is because your perception is creating a block between the supply and the flow towards you. So what does God do in order to make sure we have access to the supply? He makes us lie down in green pastures; He leads us beside quiet waters, He restores our souls, and He guides us in the paths of righteousness for His name's sake.

Let's talk about the phrase, "He leads me." I like the Hebrew terminology here. In the Hebrew, it means that he ***cajoles*** me. You know cajoling does not mean forcing. Originally, the word was used to mean guiding and helping someone by gestures of kindness to get them where they're going, to encourage them to move in a certain direction. We need to allow God to guide us so that we can access abundance. Let's talk about guidance for a second. Guidance is not forcing. God doesn't force you to go to where the supply is The way God works is by showing you stuff, so in order for you to be able to know where the supply is, your eyes have to be opened. Remember Abraham on the mountain? The bible says, "On the mountain the Lord is seen." (Gen. 22:14) The Hebrew text says that Abraham called that place Jehovah Yireh. Do you recall from our discussion in the previous chapter that Jehovah Yireh does not mean the Lord shall provide, but rather the Lord will see to it or I will see to it. So he named the place Jehovah Yireh which means on the mountain it shall be seen. This means that the key to provision is in our capacity to see. Think of it this way. The reality is provision is all around you. The reality is people are making money and making wealth every day. The reality is there are principles and there are technologies and there are things being traded every day, but if you can see, it doesn't matter. If you can't see it, you're not going to access it. So maybe what we need to do is learn how to actually see. Why is this important? Seeing is important because it is seeing that confirms, affirms, and solidifies the spiritual things into material things.

The same principle applies in the quantum realm: is light a wave or is it a particle? It depends on whose looking at it! What God wants you to do is to look with the eyes of faith. Faith changes your situation to something that you can handle. How you see really matters. If you see nothing, nothing will be there. If, when you are looking for God's supply, you say you don't see anything, then that's what you're going to get. Let me ask you this. The Bible says you are blessed if you can believe without seeing, right? (John 20:29) If you're saying, "Until I see it I won't believe it" then you need to see it so you can believe it. You don't need to see it in the physical; you need to see it in the spiritual. If seeing is believing to you, then you need to pray to see. If seeing really is your problem, then what you need to ask God to do is to let you see because if you see even in your inner being, if you see in your mind's eye, if you see in the spirit, if you see in your soul, then you're going to believe. And if you believe, then nothing is impossible to him that believes!

Everything in you that God put in you is meant to attract abundance.

There are many ways to see. Let's say you don't have spiritual insight, you have feeling sight (Not everybody sees spiritual stuff, but everybody can feel something when it's around them.) Now you use your feeling as sight and train yourself to feel abundance because if you can feel abundance, you could probably see it. The problem is we feel poverty, we feel lack, and we train ourselves to feel it as we tell ourselves stories about how everything is finished, how there's no money in the house, how there's nothing in the cupboard, how there's no food in the house, and so on. But what if you begin to train yourself to feel abundance? Some people tell us that what we feel, the universe bends to give us because we attract it to ourselves.

Everything in you that God put in you is meant to attract abundance. You may misuse what God put in you. The origin of that is not evil, but if it is actually used right, it will attract what you need in life. Your feeling is magnetic! Some of the older generation used to spend time developing what they call their "magnetic personality." What they're really doing is feeling what they desire. One of the best ways to do that is to take passages of Scripture that deal with abundance and speak it to yourself so your physical body can feel it. You feel it by putting your voice to it. We have a lot available to us. We're not like the ancients now who had to speak into walls and have it echo back to them. You know one reason most of the cathedrals were built is so that when you speak, the sound echoes back to you and your body vibrates a certain frequency that allows you to access something. These echoes in cathedrals is not just noise. They produced a vibrational frequency so that as the sound of your voice hits the walls or ceiling, it bounces back to your body. Now in this modern period, take all those passages of abundance and increase and overflow, and then with your best voice and with your joyful voice and with your faithful voice, record it to yourself and listen to it while you sleep. You don't need my voice; you need your own voice. When you feel something it affects everything. Pray to see. There are so many places in scripture where people pray for something and God opens their eyes, and they see. Haggai. Saul. Jacob. Abraham. Abraham looked behind him and saw the lamb. So he looks and he sees and he takes it. This is incredible stuff! But we're still missing something. Generation after generation after generation, the Jews were the poor people—the poorest people on earth. Do you know why? Because God spent 40 years showing them the wealth of heaven, something that a Jew can see the cause of. You can do the same thing. God brought you from heaven so you have the capacity to see the things of heaven. You have the capacity to see the fullness of what is there.

God calls you to open your eyes.

In the next verse, David says, "He guides me in paths of righteousness."

I've heard people say He leads me in the path, but it's not a single path.

The way is one, but the paths are many. Jesus listed some of them for us in the ten Beatitudes. There are more if you look at all of Jesus's commandment in Matthew chapters 5, 6, and 7. There are about thirty-two ways Jesus asked us to behave, but he wasn't saying these things just so you can do something; He gave us a way of accessing fullness because our whole teaching is about God will supply. We separate the beatitudes from the rest of the commandments in Matthew because we are overly influenced by the chapter and verse. Verse 1: I'm going to the mountain; verse two: I'm now going to talk; verse three: now I'm going to give you a beatitude. But remember that this is one whole teaching. And when you take it as a whole, it's really all about living out of the fullness of God, living out of the fullness of heaven. For instance, "Blessed are the poor in spirit for they shall inherit the earth." In fact, all the parables are all about business and accessing overflow and abundance.

In many of the parables, the pattern is that a man sees something, he finds it, and then he sees it. God calls you to open your eyes. He wants to lead you by showing you how to open your eyes. We have a saying in Nigeria: Shine your eye! It's telling you to wake up and see what is really going on. Your eyes are important. So don't just shine your physical eyes—shine your spiritual eyes, shine the eyes of your soul, shine the eyes of your body, and listen carefully to how the Lord is leading you in all those dimensions.

So God leads me in the paths of righteousness. I know there are paths of righteousness, but do you know in the scripture righteousness is tied to prosperity? I know what you're thinking, "I'm not righteous" Oh, everybody knows that! You know that, I know that, I know that about myself, but your definition of righteous is not God's definition of righteous. Walking on Paths of righteousness does not mean that you do everything right. Notice in Isaiah 35:8, God says that He will build a highway and not even the lame or fools will err or go astray from it. If it was dependent on you doing everything right, then you're going to wait forever! Get that out of your head for now because paths of righteousness is actually a path of attachment and love for God. There are many, many, many of these paths. Proverbs 8:1-3 says,

Does not wisdom call, and understanding [a]lift up her voice?
[2] On top of the heights beside the way,
Where the paths meet, she takes her stand;
[3] Beside the gates, at the opening to the city,
At the entrance of the doors, she cries out (NASB)

When you start reading through the text, Solomon says that if you listen to his voice, you're going to have riches and wealth. What is the crown of a wise man? Wealth. What is your wisdom? When God brought His commands to Israel, Moses said, "For this is your wisdom." Wait a minute—Wisdom is a person, right? Wisdom is both a woman and a man. I can say that from Scripture that Wisdom says she's a woman. Wisdom is referred to as "she." Wisdom is your first consult. Wisdom knew you before your DNA was put on earth. So Wisdom is a woman. However, then the Bible turns around and says, "Jesus Christ, the wisdom of God." (1 Cor. 1:30) Wisdom is both son and mother! Wisdom is the reason that Jesus said to John when He was on the cross, "Behold your mother! Woman, behold your son!" The reason Wisdom talks like that, according to the ancients, because she is always pregnant with abundance. We say our wisdom is a practical idea of ordering things to come to pass. Wisdom is no such thing because Wisdom is not building anything in the book of Proverbs. Wisdom prays in the presence of God! Wisdom plays and dances in the presence of God.

True wisdom is enjoying what God does, but you can't enjoy what God does if you're concerned about what God hasn't done. Wisdom is not the thing we keep saying it is. We even put the word "practical" in front of wisdom, don't we? Read Proverbs 8:22-31 again:

"The LORD possessed me at the beginning of His way,
Before His works of old.
From everlasting I was established,
From the beginning, from the earliest times of the earth.
"When there were no depths I was brought forth,
When there were no springs abounding with water.
"Before the mountains were settled,
Before the hills I was brought forth;
While He had not yet made the earth and the fields,
Nor the first dust of the world.
"When He established the heavens, I was there,
When He inscribed a circle on the face of the deep,
When He made firm the skies above,
When the springs of the deep became fixed,
When He set for the sea its boundary
So that the water would not transgress His command,
When He marked out the foundations of the earth;
Then I was beside Him, as a master workman;
And I was daily His delight,
Rejoicing always before Him,
Rejoicing in the world, His earth,
And having my delight in the sons of men.

Wisdom rejoiced when there was nothing there, and She rejoiced and danced whenever He created something. She was there when He put a circle on nothingness, and she watched and rejoiced with Him. She rejoiced with the sons of men before they were on the earth. Real Wisdom enjoys what God has done or what God is doing—not complaining about what God is not doing.

> Ask God to give you sight to see where your abundance is located. You might be shocked to realize that God points back to you.

So one of the paths of righteousness is a path of interconnection between you and God. This path that leads to complete abundance through you enjoying and rejoicing in what God does.

The reason for our continuous lack, poverty, and limitation is that we don't value what's been given to us. We're constantly looking for something, and we don't realize that the joy we bring to what is present is what causes the open door to increase. For example, if you give children a penny or a dollar, they are very happy. But if you give their friend a dollar, they forget that they have a dollar and start fighting for their friend's dollar. We can behave that way as well. We think ours is not enough, The idea that you are the key to your own breakthrough, prosperity, and abundance is solidly biblical.

Ask God to give you sight to see where your abundance is located. You might be shocked to realize that God points back to you. Learn how to see what is inside of you. Secondly, get Wisdom. When I talk about getting Wisdom, I'm not talking about learning how to craft something. You can learn that later on. I want you to get wisdom by doing exactly what Wisdom did in the presence of love: rejoice in what you have and speak well of what you have. If you do this, then what you have will give up its fragrance to you. All you need is a seed. You don't need the whole world. Just sing over it. Rejoice over it even in the midst of chaos.

In this season, God spoke to me saying, "I want to expose my people to a heart of abundance." He didn't tell me He is going to give you money; He told me, "I will expose them to a heart of abundance." I think that's important. The world is not running out. There's always enough for you too. It's not going to be gone before it's your turn. God didn't create you and say that when this person comes into the world, all my abundance will stop. He never did that. You carry the same abundance whatever you are facing. Whatever you're facing now is just a bump in the road and it's meant to shock you into the next level of your abundance. What should you do? Focus your mind on the abundance. Let your feeling receive the abundance. Celebrate what is in your hands. Just celebrate it! I do not mean be lazy. Laziness is a disease that people need to be cured of. A lazy person can't praise and worship God for what is present because it takes all your strength and power to do so. It takes strength not to complain when everything in you is saying complain. It takes strength to rejoice in the midst of what seems like nothing is going right. The person who is worshiping and celebrating God in what they have is actually a strong person.

Chapter 4

WALKING IN THE SHADOW

Psalm 23 teaches the principle of provision and overflowing possibilities.

But then we come to verse 4:

Even though I walk through the valley of the shadow of death.
I fear no evil. For you are with me;
Your rod and Your staff. They comfort me. (NASB)

...How do we as believers still operate under this principle of abundance in the context of the shadow of death?

There is a shadow that keeps us from or even kills the flow of divine wealth, divine prosperity, divine overflow and abundance in our lives. When David says I walk through the valley of the shadow of death, he is actually quoting Job. Job uses the phrase "shadow of death" at least five times in a very negative way to mean "the shadow of my life is disappearing" Why? In Job's way of thinking, a shadow is a fleeting thing, temporary and shifting. It is not a constant. It's something dark that you can't get a handle on. In the tradition that I grew up in, we talk about the tree of life and we talk about shadow trees. Shadows, or "shade" as the English use to call them, are like demons. I don't want to dwell on demons, but here is the point. You get into a position where you are in line for the flow of the prosperity or the fundamental nature of the shepherd, the flow of the shepherd's heart and all that comes with it. You're in line for receiving that which comes out of rest and then shifting events come into your life that are meant to create certain attitude, Ideas, or responses that hinder your capacity to receive what is flowing from your shepherd into your life. So when David proclaims, "Even though I walk through the valley of the shadow of death, I will fear no evil," it means it's not really necessary for you to be in the shadow of death. Why? Because God has already told you your position.

Read these verses again:

The Lord is my shepherd,
I shall not want.
He makes me lie down in green pastures;
He leads me beside quiet waters.
He restores my soul;
He guides me in the paths of righteousness
For His name's sake.

He's already told you your position. You don't have to stay in the valley of the shadow of death.

In Ephesians 1:3, it says,

Blessed be the God and Father of our Lord Jesus Christ, *who has blessed us with every spiritual blessing in the heavenly places in Christ* (NASB)

This world is not a world of shadow. Shadows move according to the position of light. If there is a shadow, you have to ask which kind of shadow is it and where the light is positioned to cast the shadow.

There is a shadow of death and there is a shadow of life. There is the shadow of the wing of God. Are you getting the point now? The type of shadow depends on which type of light it is coming from. The shadow of death is the result of a false light that is thrown upon your life to draw your eyes and your mind away from the first three verses of Psalm 23 where you already seated. When you are in the valley of the shadow of death, you have to realize that the shadow is thrown by a false kind of light.

> If you begin to depend on something other than that which is established in the spiritual realm, you create a false shadow upon yourself.

Let's talk about some of the different sources of false light. You know God wants to prosper you. God has all that you need. He wants to work in your life. You know he is not holding anything back from you. However, when certain circumstances arise, you begin to believe transient issues, conditions, things that people say to you, and things you say to yourself. Here's the thing—people will say nice things to you one minute and terrible things the next. Then you begin to depend on predictions of the economy and all negative things that could happen in the world. If you begin to depend on something other than that which is established in the spiritual realm, you create a false shadow upon yourself. Those shadows kill. The first thing that the shadow kills is your concentration and your focus on what you already know. How does it do that? By creating doubt. Doubt is a shadow of death. What does this mean? If doubt is the shadow of death, then faith is a shadow of light. Faith is something that says, "even though I walk through the valley of the shadow of death, I will not fear evil.

Let's focus for a minute on walking. One of the ways to overcome false shadows and to change shadows is to keep moving. Never get stuck and never allow yourself to be so stuck in what has happened to you. It will kill you. It will destroy you. Part of dealing with the shadow of death is to keep walking and keep moving.

> Being stuck in the valley of the shadow of death produces the shadow of blame.

Next we have to deal with fear. Where there is doubt, fear will surely follow. And what does fear do? Both doubt and fear will keep you stuck in the valley of the shadow of death. When I read David saying, "though I walk through the valley of the shadow of death," I ask myself what are those shadows? He lists them for us. Doubt is a shadow. Fear is a shadow. We talk about the lack of vision as a shadow, which is actually blindness. Proverbs 29:18 says, "Where there is no vision, the people perish." (KJV) So when you lack vision, not only are you blind, you are in the valley of the shadow of death.

Lack of vision throws you into a spiraling abyss. What will happen if I'm stuck in the valley of the shadow of Death. If I'm doubting and I have fear and I don't have a vision, what will happen? My tendency would be to find out who is it that is stopping me from being able to move. One thing about being stuck in the shadow of the valley of the shadow of death is that it doesn't allow you to see who you are, either in the positive or in the negative sense. When people talk about themselves in a negative sense, they are actually looking for someone to blame. People say, "Why do I do this or why am I in this situation?" Of course, the big boogie man is the devil. We know that already because he's the one who gets all the blame. Some people even blame God.

Being stuck in the valley of the shadow of death produces the shadow of blame. Whose fault is this? Not mine! It cannot possibly be mine!

When I walk through the valley of the shadow of death, what keeps me from fearing evil? Verse 4 says, "for ***You*** are with me; Your rod and Your staff, they comfort me." In the Hebrew, "You" is written as Atta **(אתה)** and is a reference to God's name.

You [are] > 'at·tāh > **אַתָּה**

In Old English, Atta is translated as Thou, which is a reference for royalty. When we say "You" today, it is a common reference that could be used for anyone. However, in this instance, the "You" carries this meaning of royalty and respect.

David says that the reason I can deal with the shadows is because Atta is with me—Aleph, Tav, Heh**(אתה)** . If you remove the Heh, you are left with Aleph Tav which is the Alpha and Omega. The Alpha, because it comes at the beginning of Atta, opens an otherwise closed system. In other words, the reason why I'm not afraid is because I am in a system that's always open for possibility. Because Atta is with me, possibility is with me. There is another shadow called **[foreign 1:20:15]** or in the Hebrew **[foreign 1:20:18].** The bible says in Psalm 91,

He who dwells in the secret place of the Most High
Shall abide under the shadow of the Almighty. (NKJV)

Let's look again at the Hebrew for "I will fear no evil" which is pronounced "Lo yi ra ra."

rā'	'î·rā	lō-
רָא	יִרָא	לֹא
evil	I will fear	no

Notice that "yi ra" is a combination of the Yod Resh and Aleph and the word for evil is Resh Aleph. The addition of the Yod indicates that this is the hand of God and standing over evil.. "Ra" is evil but "yira" is to stand above evil. So I can walk through the valley of the shadow of death and not fear evil because Atta is with me. And because there are open possibilities before me, I can keep moving forward. I understand that I will never get stuck because I understand Who is with me. Not only is Atta with me, His rod and His staff comfort me.

Let's talk about the rod and staff. Really these are two pillars in the House of God that He uses to comfort me: number one is mercy and the other one is strength. His mercy and strength are the reasons for my comfort.

yenachamuni	<u>heimmah</u>
יְנַחֲמֻנִי	הֵמָּה
comfort me	they

I can remember Atta is with me, providing open possibilities with mercy on my right hand and strength on my left. Strength and mercy are not going to comfort me in the future—they create a position of rest for me right now. Remember the goal: the only way I can receive what the Father has already spoken in the beginning of Psalm 23 is by coming to a place of rest. So when I am in the context of the shadow of death, I must still find myself in a position of rest because the reason all these shadows come is to shift me away from rest, making it impossible for me to receive what actually belongs to me. Because of agitation, I miss my moments.

We've got to learn to stay in this position of rest, especially now in the world in which we find ourselves, where greedy and powerful men are trying to create a system of fear. Whether we like it or not. Whether we are evangelical or Pentecostal or anything else, we are walking in the valley of the shadow of death. There is a lot of stuff that is coming up in the world, but a believer cannot allow these circumstances to keep them from understanding that Atta is always present. For the believer, mercy and strength are always present and provide comfort and rest. It is this comfort and rest which allows the believer to receive in the midst of agitation, to prosper even in the midst of the valley of the shadow of death, and to bring forth life even where there is death.

Thy rod and thy staff they comfort me! These shadows are not permanent. They are temporal—especially the shadow of death. The only shadow that is permanent is under the wing of God. It is a shadow of El Shaddai. El Shaddai is a name of provision. This means that if I'm under the shadow of El Shaddai, I'm actually living under perfect light. The funny thing about the shadow of the Father is that it is a shadow of light. It is not a shadow of doubt, a shadow of darkness, or a shadow of destruction.

It says in Psalm 121:5:

The Lord is your keeper;
The Lord is your shade on your right hand.

Since God is light, we know that David is not talking about the same shadow as in Psalm 23. Can you imagine light hitting me and my shadow, instead of being something that blocks light, its actually like bright light? That's precisely what David is saying. So being in the shadow of the wing of God transfers God's light into your circumstance. It is a second shadow, so to speak, that flows into your context when you are in the valley of the shadow of death. In other words, you always have another shadow there but that shadow itself is light. It almost seems contradictory, but it is still light. It's a clear, translucent manifestation of divinity in the context of your darkness.

I will not fear any evil for thou art with me;
thy rod and thy staff they comfort me.

Comfort and rest are the basis of miracles.

"Comfort, yes, comfort My people!" Says your God.
"Speak comfort to Jerusalem, and cry out to her
That her warfare is ended,
That her iniquity is pardoned..." (Isaiah 40:1-2a, NKJV)

When God talks about comfort in this context, He is saying that no matter what one is going through, the trials are already past, the pain that came before is already healed. God says to tell her that her warfare is over. God is speaking comfort to you in the context of your suffering. It means your suffering is already done.

So when a word of comfort comes to you, accept that you are already delivered from the situation. Otherwise, God would not speak comfort to you, right? Comfort is a harbinger of good news. Isaiah 40:9 says:

O Zion,
You who bring good tidings,
Get up into the high mountain;
O Jerusalem,
You who bring good tidings,
Lift up your voice with strength,
Lift it up, be not afraid;
Say to the cities of Judah, "Behold your God!" (NKJV)

When the word of comfort comes and when Jesus says, "They shall be comforted," it means that there's always a flow of good news and a flow of open possibility in the context of what you're going through. Don't say you're not going to be in the shadow, but if you get in the shadow you don't really have to be. A lot of the shadows we walk in, we walk into ourselves. If you are in the context of the valley of the shadow of death, you have to understand that, since Atta is with you, there's mercy, there's strength, and there's comfort. And comfort means that there's good news in the context of your suffering. The good news is that God has already made the decision that your future is present in the context of that shadow. God does not leave you in the shadow. He comforts you to bring you out of the valley of the shadow of death and into the shadow of His wing, the valley of the shadow of the Almighty. He's telling you to stand on your feet and let's go home.

I'm learning that God doesn't wait for the situation to be over to comfort you.

I'm learning that God doesn't wait for the situation to be over to comfort you. You can see it in the way God dealt with Job. He visited Job while Job was suffering. The suffering was not over before God came to Job. The thing is God was already there looking at Job. He was already there comforting Job through Elihu (Job 32-38) God, Atta, was present in the context of Job's suffering.

I love the word "Atta" (**אַתָּה**)! I have spent a lot of time with that word. Aleph is the principle of creation that God put for Himself in order to have an ace to remove the world from every condition into which it enters. For Atta, it means that, not only is the Aleph of the precreation principle present, but the Aleph of the future world is present as well.

Let me encourage you—whatever it is that you're going through, there is no valley of the shadow where Atta is not present. There's nothing you go through where there is no open possibility. You are the open possibility. That's what you are. You can never be enclosed so much so that you can't come out. There's no way given who you are as a child of God. Remember who is with you. Can you catch the wind? Can you hold heaven and bind it with the string? Can you take God and make Him your prisoner? If you cannot, then it is impossible for you to be held captive such that you cannot get out. It may be a little long, but just hold on. Hold on a little while longer. It's going to be alright. I promise it's going to be alright because your God will not fail you. This is not the end of your life. It can never be. There's always an opening and there is always a comfort for you. God's comfort means that your future has already come to your present. Amen.

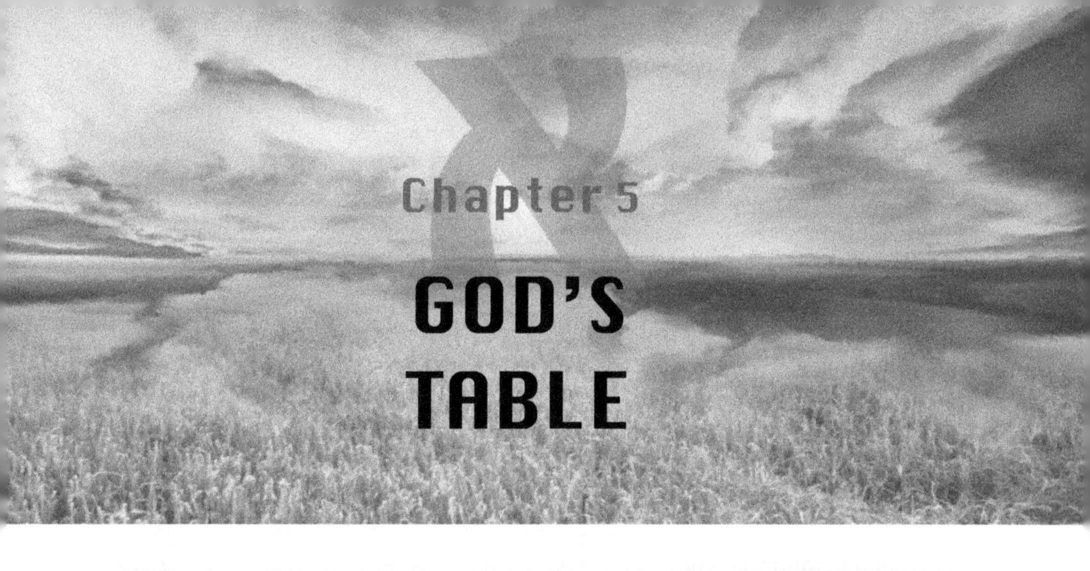

Chapter 5

GOD'S TABLE

> We continue with the text in Psalm 23:5
> You prepare a table before me in the presence of my enemies (NASB)

We are dealing with this idea of supernatural provision and the overwhelming flow of God's providence towards those who are his children. I'm not a prosperity preacher, but I believe in wealth, I believe that the struggle believers have has to do with operating from the place of lack in everything. Operating from lack is what makes us compare ourselves with one another. It's what makes us think something is being taken away from us. When we operate from the perspective that something is being taken away from us, we cease and we are unable to actually harvest the fullness of what is in the present. We must all learn to believe that being blessed means living in the fullness of who God is. God is blessed, not because we give Him blessing—God is blessed because it is His intrinsic personality.

When we bless God and speak well of Him, we activate the fullness of God and release it to flow through us. We add nothing to God; we take nothing from God. The believer must come to the point where they are so full and they understand the fullness of themselves, they don't feel like something is being taken away from them because somebody comes into their presence. This is a very important Christian principle, but it is hard for people to learn because we are taught our whole lives that people who come into our life are trying to take something away from us. However, no matter how you couch it, no matter how much religion or spirituality you put on it, it is not Christian to respond this way. Nothing is being taken away from you. We have to change this way of thinking because it leads to serious problems in both our personal lives and society. When we operate from this faulty perspective, it means we don't believe in the ever-flowing fullness of God to which we are connected. We've been trained as a society to believe that the universe is based on fundamental lack - not on fundamental plenitude - so we bite each other, beat each other, hurt each other, and fight with each other because we think something is being taken away from us. We must understand that the God who created the universe doesn't suffer lack. The universe is based on fundamental plenitude, fundamental purification, and a fundamental capacity to reproduce, to restore, to rectify, to reunify, and to heal itself. It's a completely different perspective.

We must understand that the God who created the universe doesn't suffer lack.

What happens in relationships if we approach them from the perspective of lack? There can never be any real trust because we are always expecting that the other person just wants to take something from us. Not only that, we will end up trying to benefit or "be on top" in the relationship by drawing from the other person's fullness in spite of their weakness. Can you see how operating from lack leads to the corruption of our own motives and intent as well?

When David declares, "Thou prepares a table before me," he is not just telling us what God is providing for us. He also reminded us of the protocol of God's table and how we must prepare ourselves to come to the table. There's a book that was written in 1563 by Joseph Karo, one of the great rabbis, called **Shulcan Aruch** which means "the preparation of the table." It is five volumes concerning the law, how to prepare yourself to keep the law, and how to prepare yourself to preach. One of the things that makes Jews different is that we spend a lot of time preparing ourselves to worship. Some call it religious; we call it preparation. We have to be careful of how we use the word "religious." Every time somebody prepares themselves to do something for God, many Christians have the tendency to call it religious. If somebody says you should practice a spiritual activity, you say it's "religious." If somebody says you should prepare for coming before God, you say it's "religious." You're invited to pray five times a day, but you won't do it because you see it as a superficial, meaningless, "religious" activity. Would you invite the King to a table without preparation because you don't want to be religious? This is what we've done to ourselves—we've freed ourselves from actually engaging God in His fullness by calling everything we do "religious." Yet these are the very things that actually activate the fullness of God in our lives! I'm of the opinion that this whole language about things being religious is from the devil not from God because it stops believers from doing what they're supposed to do to access the fullness of who they are. We become our own worst enemies by condemning the very things that empower our own spiritual growth. And we call it spirituality!

When we operate from lack and the perspective that an enemy must always be an enemy, we want to eat alone and make sure our enemies have nothing to eat.

I like the word ta'aroch shulcan which means "You prepare a table." This table is an amazing thing because it is prepared facing me in my presence. However, there's no place that says the table is prepared *for* me. Many interpretations of Psalm 23:5 say that God has prepared a table *for* me *in front of* my enemy so my enemies can watch me eating. But what if the table is prepared before me in the presence of my enemy for the purpose of my enemies participating with me and being transformed? What if God's table is a divine transmutation or principle whereby all are invited to participate and be transformed? Think about how Jesus tells us to treat our enemies. He tells us to love our enemies and to pray for them when they curse us (Matthew 5:44). Paul, quoting Proverbs, said to feed our enemy if he is hungry (Romans 12:20). When we operate from lack and the perspective that an enemy must always be an enemy, we want to eat alone and make sure our enemies have nothing to eat. We want to make sure that those who are more wicked than we are cannot participate at God's table as if this makes us righteous. I think the idea of ta'aroch shulcan is extremely important here. Preparing ourselves and the practice of preparation is transmutational because it speaks of God's deliberate intention. When God prepares this table, He intentionally does so. He does not throw food on the table in front of someone haphazardly. This same God who prepares the table before me is the same God who provides even for the world, even for my enemies.

If God prepares His table out of the fullness of His being, He must be preparing it so that all who are around me can benefit from it.

I think we have a perspective in life that is so colored by society and our ideology, we don't have the capacity usually to step outside and look at these types of things objectively. We think our enemies must always suffer, but God did not treat us that way. The bible says while we were yet enemies of God, we were reconciled to Him through Christ's death (Romans 5:10). If the interpretation of Psalm 23:5 is God prepares food so I can eat and my enemies can suffer, then why did God invite me to participate at His table while I was still His enemy? God prepared a table in front of Israel so that you, even as an enemy, can partake and become whole! This is where our ideology goes awry. Even though we preach the fullness of the Holy Spirit and the fullness of sanctification, we still don't understand that fullness must overflow even to our enemies.

This means that when I'm eating in the presence of God, my enemies are in the presence of God with me. I bring them with me. My eating with God must include my enemies because it is in my fellowship with God that they become transmuted. If I leave them out, there is nowhere they can get changed. How can we change the world when we eat alone? This is why Christianity is difficult. This is why growing a church and having a fellowship is difficult—because your enemies must participate in spite of themselves. You must include them. Perhaps we want to have a type of Christianity where our enemies are far away, but our job is to create a world where there are no enemies. How do we do that—by keeping our enemies afar or by bringing them in to participate in the fellowship? Love is a transmutational key, isn't it? Jesus said love can change anybody. In fact, the preparation of the table in the presence of my enemy is a transmutational key that exemplifies God's intrinsic nature and how we can be like Him.

> God does not bless me so that my enemies can eat their heart out.

Let's talk about our internal enemies that live inside of us. Do you not eat with all those enemies that are inside of you? You don't wait till they are removed before you eat. God teaches us a lot about how He deals with us when David says, "Thou preparest a table before me." The Hebrew word is lefenay **(לְפָנַי)** and literally means in front of me or in my face. This is usually translated as "before me," but it actually should be translated "towards my face." In this case, the actual participation in the table is a face-to-face encounter with the enemy. How do you transform an enemy if you are unwilling to talk with them face-to-face? It doesn't matter how it goes. Until you encounter them face-to-face, you can't change them.

As we meditate on this verse, what we need to remember is God's table is not a personal, private table. It's actually a public table because your enemies are around it as well. God's table is transformational and transmutational. God prepares it. It is His table, not mine or yours. Through the transmutational nature of His love, He gives you the permission to participate.

God prepares His table right in front of you, in your face, so that you can participate in His banquet and when your enemies witness this, they themselves will also be transformed.

Everything He is doing for you, He's doing for the salvation of the world to turn all of us around.

God does not bless me so that my enemies can eat their heart out. He blesses me so my enemies can see how good He is and turn in repentance to Him. We must understand this God operates from position of fullness, not lack. Everything He is doing for you, He's doing for the salvation of the world to turn all of us around.

אתה

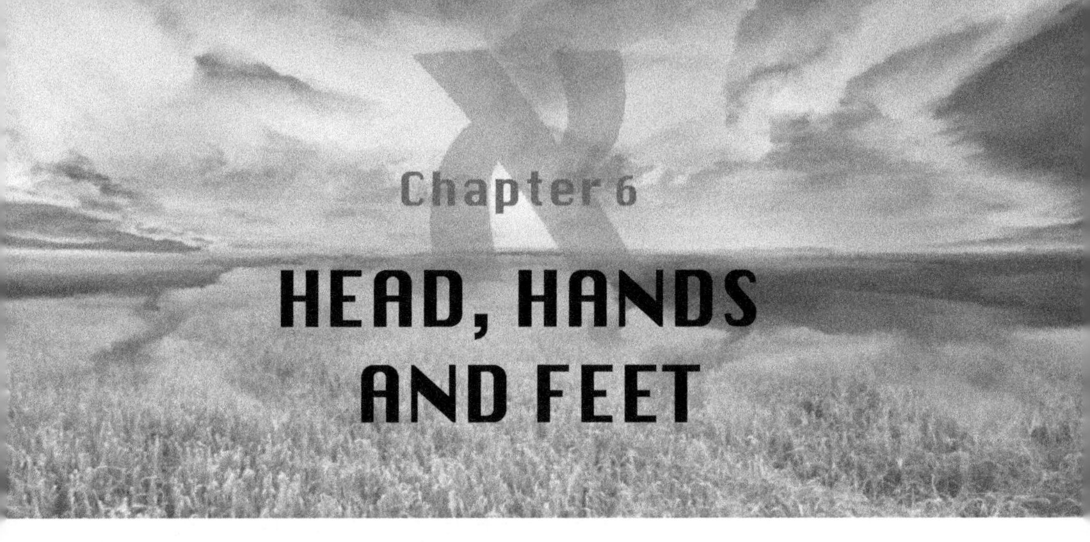

Chapter 6

HEAD, HANDS AND FEET

We have dealt with 'the table' in the previous chapter. Let's look at "Thou anointest my head with oil, my cup runneth over.

I want to combine the two. We spirit-filled believers with all our prophetic and evangelistic and charismatic perspectives have a lot to say about anointing. The word for "anoint" that is used here is the word deshanta. It means to make fat, to cause to expand, to cause to completely purify. The word deshanta has the same root as the Mashiach, which is the anointed one or messiah. However, the structure of deshanta is different than Mashiach I think David used this word very deliberately.

When you call somebody the anointed one, you're talking about the person being given a load or something being put upon them that allows the person to bear whatever is coming their way. In other words, the anointed one is given a seed that brings forth a purpose. However, when we talk about Thou anointest my head with oil, it is important that we understand why it is the *head* that is being anointed—literally, rubs the oil upon my head. In one of the Jewish books on mysticism, called the *Likkutei Amarim*, it says that there is a soul in the human brain and that this soul contains the Chabad, which is wisdom, understanding, and knowledge. When David speaks about this whole issue of walking in abundance, he is saying that the head, or rosh **(רֹאשׁ)** is important for the opening of abundance. How your head works determines whether you prosper or whether you don't. If you give a fool wealth they'll squander it (Proverbs 21:20). This was Solomon's complaint. He was doing all this work and didn't know if the one he was going to leave it to was going to be a fool or a wise person.

By the end of this chapter, you will see that Psalm 23 is really about an overflowing, super abundant life. Why does David focus on anointing the head? The idea of deshanta is to fatten and grow. It is the anointing of kings that is always done on the head. In addition to kings and priests, God instructs the Jews to anoint ordinary things and smear them with oil like sticks, the tabernacle, altars, Aaron's garments, even the utensils of the tabernacle. Sometimes the word can also be used for the removal of ashes that have been burnt upon an altar.

The idea of anointing is a powerful thing, Anointing readies the person or object for the reception of the glory and the intention of God in Whose presence a person stands or in Whose presence an object is used.

The idea of anointing is a powerful thing, Anointing readies the person or object for the reception of the glory and the intention of God in Whose presence a person stands or in Whose presence an object is used. Without the anointing, it cannot receive the glory and the purpose of the One in whose presence it is supposed to be manifest. So the anointing is given first of all to make the person a place, or to make the person usable or ready for the entrance of the glory because the anointing without the glory is nothing but oil making something oily.

The anointing is always for God's purpose. David says that the anointing in this case is only on the head because the intellectual process is important to God for making a person prosperous. Anointing is more than just praying and asking God to do a miracle. The way you use your head determines whether you prosper or not.

As Pentecostals, we have not taught people how to use their heads to make wealth. We've taught them how to use their knees to make wealth. As we have seen, the head contains three things: the left brain, the right brain, and the soul which is wisdom, understanding, and knowledge. This means that the brain serves as a funnel for the entrance of things from the supernatural realm into this realm. We deceive ourselves if we think we're actually going to transform people if we don't expect people to think in church and we talk to them at the lowest common level. It's a waste of time. I have people tell me all the time that I am talking above their understanding, but I urge them to come up higher. Why must I talk to you as if you are dumb, foolish, or ignorant when I know that what is in you is greater than anything I can teach you? When David emphasizes the importance of anointing the head, he calls attention to the need to engage our intellects in this process of operating in abundance. You can't actually even be a holy person without using your intellect because holiness is making choices to do good things based on God's direction. The Jewish term is *mitzvah* which is an intentional obedience of the law and choosing to perform acts of kindness. In all these things, your brain is supposed to be involved. There is no reason why you should leave your brain in the parking lot when you come to church. It doesn't mean you stand there and argue all the time because you won't get anything out of that, but allow your brain to function. Your soul and your brain working together is what takes in the intent of your heart and makes it functional through your hand. In other words, the intent of your heart never comes to pass until you engage the soul. The reason God anoints your head is because it is the magnetic point at which the supernatural realm enters into your being.

Revelation is a combination of wisdom, understanding, and knowledge.

We talk a lot about the heart, but we don't talk about the head, and we became all sentimental in church. When you engage some Christians intellectually, they get offended and so what happens then is they don't know how to be challenged. When they go into the world and there are structures and patterns and paradigms on doing things they don't want to engage, they want a shortcut so that they can be successful in areas about in which they have never thought. They want a miracle so they don't have to think about it or figure it out. That does not mean that your rationalistic process solves anything. The reason for the anointing is to combine your intellectual process with your God given wisdom, understanding, and knowledge.

I am not just talking about the information-gathering process whereby you collect and then analyze the data. You must bring data, information, and divine revelation all together. You cannot eliminate one piece of this equation. The problem is some people have data and that's all they have. Some people have lots of hearsay and that's all they have. Some people even think they have revelation, although if it's not combined with knowledge, I don't know how they can call it revelation. How can you have revelation without information? If God gives you revelation, He's also going to give you the necessary information to support it.

Revelation is a combination of wisdom, understanding, and knowledge. Knowledge is the result of combining facts, information, and data. For example, a baby is born by knowledge. The bible says Adam *knew* his wife (Genesis 4:1). There are two people involved, the father and the mother, along with wisdom and understanding to produce this knowledge. The baby is a manifestation of the knowledge of the father and the mother. According to some of my great rabbis, it is the brain of the father that conceives the baby before the semen gets into the mother's womb and then he plants that seed. The baby is not just a result of a physical act. The baby is the manifestation of a cognitive process that gets activated in the brain of the man, that then releases and goes into the woman, it sits there for nine months, and comes out as knowledge. It is a very powerful thing to look at your children and realize that you're looking at the consummation of knowledge and wisdom and understanding that started from another realm that came as an anointing upon your head.

Anointing is a way to expand you to be able to handle what you have been given to do.

Deshanta can also mean to remove the burnt ashes on the altar. So when an anointing comes upon you, it de-clutters your mind. If you say you have anointing and your mind is cluttered with mess that's not an anointing. Part of the process of anointing is for your mind and your brain to become de-cluttered and for the ashes of generations of bad thinking to be clean. Let's take David, for example. David was really from a line of incest. From what we read from Scripture, David is a great man, but something about his father's relationship with his mom wasn't right. However, the anointing removes that and opens some new vistas of understanding about who David is, his relationship with the world, and what he's supposed to accomplish. Another good example is Jesus Christ himself, here is a young man born from a woman who says she saw an angel. What would happen if your daughter came to you and said she saw an angel? I know what I would say: "Show me the guy." That's what the Jews did until Jesus died. They said, "Show us your father. Is this not the Son of Mary or Joseph the carpenter?" They had words for Him. Forget the fact that Jesus was God as a human being. It must have been hard to walk around town and hear people, especially because we know that Jesus knew what they were thinking and what was in their hearts. So can you imagine Jesus walking around and, for His whole life, hearing people say, "Yeah, right! His mother saw an angel! It must be one of the Roman soldiers that was the angel." However, because of the anointing, those things never took ascendancy in his life and you never hear Jesus talk about it. He focuses his mind so that it is clear from the clutter of human conversation about his identity. Most people with that kind of background always mix their mess with their message. It's always about them because of their father's failure. Not so with Jesus Christ.

For the sake of clarity, Jesus was not anointed at birth, but at his baptism because being a son of God is not the same as being anointed. You only need anointing for certain work or for a thought process that will produce God's desired result. The anointing on the head means that His consciousness is being expanded to be able to handle the greatness of the desire and the thought of God for his life. So the anointing is the expansion of your consciousness and your capacity to receive from the fullness of who God is in your life. Therefore, if God says He wants to use you to change the world, you can't handle it ordinarily unless God brings something that expands your capacity to handle that.

Thus, anointing is a way to expand you to be able to handle what you have been given to do. Then when you finish handling the task for which God has anointed you, you can't do it anymore because the anointing created an expansiveness, a capacity for you to handle the greater responsibility for the moment. Consequently, you should never boast about it because the anointing is not yours. If you receive an anointing for speaking, everybody thinks you're wonderful until it gets to your head. You might think it's all you and then the anointing lifts and people see your human frailties. Nevertheless, the anointing will actually beautify you because in doing so, it allows people to listen to the things you are saying and they might not listen to you if the anointing is not there. Aaron was also changed by the anointing. Remember he was an idol worshiper and, more than that, he actually called Satan forth from Hell. However, when the anointing came, he became the high priest and was able to open up heaven. Even ordinary sticks that were made into utensils became carriers of divine presence once they were rubbed with the oil.

So the anointing is the expansion of your consciousness and your capacity to receive from the fullness of who God is in your life.

Real anointing does not stay on the head. It flows onto the hand. When David says, "My cup runneth over," he is saying that prosperity comes by the head and hand. Think of a cup bearer. The cup doesn't sit on the table and run over. The idea is that the cup is tipped or *bent* to release what is in it. The word for cup in Hebrew is kavas**(כּוֹס)** and begins with the letter *Kaph*. Kaph can mean something that is so overwhelmingly grievous that the burden is too much to bear. However, it can also mean something that is bent to release what is in it, Kaph, like the hand, is able to carry but also to pour out.

So the significance of the cup that runs over is that it connects the hand and the head. I am writing to this generation, to those who say that they are anointed, but don't want to do the work and use their hands. Instead, they sit around, fast for 25 days, and wait for God to download a miracle. The anointing *must* flow through the cup of the hand because wealth comes from head to hand. If God wants to prosper you, He will give you an idea of what to do. He will put something in your head that works out in your hand. After the anointing came upon his hand, David said, "Blessed is the Lord that teaches my hand to work."

David is credited with making many instruments. It is not biblical that you don't have to use your hand and God will just drop things from heaven. There are times God does miracles, but you don't sit around and wait for angels to clean your house. God promised you wealth, but He promised to put ideas in your head and to strengthen your hand to bring it to pass. He put the record in the palm of your hand. Moses prayed in Psalm 90:17, "And establish the work of our hands for us; Yes, establish the work of our hands." (NKJV) " I'm getting tired of believers who want to be mystical but who refuse to work. If ideas come into your head, go and work it out. Angels will help you when you stretch your hand out, but you're sitting around waiting for things to manifest. The angel does not see the record of your scroll if you do not stretch out your hand .

Angels will help you when you stretch your hand out, but you're sitting around waiting for things to manifest.

I have people tell me all the time that they want to be like me and travel all over the world and teach. I tell them plainly that they really don't want to because they're lazy and just want to have fun. Perhaps you don't understand how I'm spending my time. I do not sit around and wait. I come home from a vacation at 3 AM and go to my office to get ready for what I'm teaching the next morning. This is not about your personal brilliance and your capacity to recount information; this is about being able to receive from heaven, having your wisdom in your brain and understanding and knowledge working together as a triangular downward funnel to bring the supernatural realm into this realm. In this way, it reaches out influencing how you do things with your hands, ten fingers, ten principles of creation, ten commandments. Life is not a lottery.

God anoints your head and He pours ideas from heaven. Every time you pray, God is speaking and downloading. You don't need a special time where God is downloading. Your Father is *always* speaking. He's giving you ideas so use your head and think. The problem is most of us listen to it and we turn it into religion. God speaks to you about how to change the world technologically and you say God is sending me to Africa because you don't want to work to make what you are doing a reality. If that is the case, God will give it to somebody else. We've got to sit down and listen to receive ideas. Get a pen and paper and write down the ideas even if they don't make sense. If it means you have to go back to school to learn how to connect wire to wire to be an electrician, do it. If it means you have to become a plumber to be able to fabricate the things that God has given you in your head, do it no matter how old you are. This is not about age. The head and the hand working as one is key to operating in abundance. Show me a thinking man that doesn't want to move their hands I will show you a man who will be rich in his head and poor in life. Show me a man who works with his hands and doesn't really think and I will show you a man who is going to be a slave to everybody else that produces. You are depending on everybody else while God has given you this brilliant mind. You have got this gift of thinking, but your hands are lazy. You've got this capacity to pray, but your hands are lazy so when the idea is sent you don't catch it because you aren't thinking. And when you do catch it, you turn it into a religion. Your hands don't want to work so it just stays in your head until somebody else catches it.

God gives you the power to make wealth

I'm sure you have had ideas that are evident in your life today, but don't make the mistake of thinking that there is no relationship between spirituality and economics. We can talk about economics religiously and how we move in and out of power, but in the end, people with money will make the decision on how things work. This doesn't mean money is your God, but God gives you the power to make wealth. It's not a miracle. It's not magic. Remember ten fingers, ten principles of creation; ten fingers, ten Beatitudes; ten fingers, Ten Commandments; ten fingers, ten trials of Abraham; ten fingers, ten plagues that moved Egypt. God keeps giving us these references to the hand of the Lord. In fact, He speaks about the hand of the Lord frequently in the book of

Exodus. Even the Egyptians recognized that it was the hand of the Lord that had come against them.

I haven't yet talked about what it means to work miracles because many of us don't understand that a miracle is actually a work. We keep thinking a miracle is just something you say and it happens. The miracle is actually a work. If a miracle happens, it means they've worked on it all night.

The tabernacle of Moses did not fall down from heaven. It was given into somebody's head who used their hands to fabricate all the tools required to build it even before Moses commanded it to stand up. God is looking for his children to become much more economically savvy because that's really where this is going. The war we fight is a spiritual war that is tied directly to economics. If we're going to operate in abundance, we have got to start using these principles and teach the next generation to do the same. There was a time in our movement when we were all waiting for it to manifest. Again, there are times when things manifest, but the biblical principle is that this kind of manifestation is a sign for what you're supposed to do. So don't use a sign as the final reality; use a sign as a pointer to what you're supposed to do. That's why they are called signs and wonders. A sign, in this case, is a pointer to what you're capable of doing. It doesn't mean that if God brings down a car from heaven that He's going to keep bringing down cars. He brought the car down so you can learn how to build it and manifest more on your own without God. That's why an unbeliever can do certain things you cannot do The unbeliever needs God for salvation but he doesn't need God to be able to create the technology because God has already given the technology. If God uses you to produce something today and it is produced from righteousness, unbelievers can still take it and duplicate it. The Chinese take all American inventions and recreate them without believing in the God you believe in. There's not one of us to whom God has not given an idea. We may have lost it because we were waiting for some magic to take place. Get yourself a piece of paper, get yourself a notebook, start drawing, start writing, start putting the ideas down. If you don't bring it to pass, somebody else will.

There's not one of us to whom God has not given an idea.

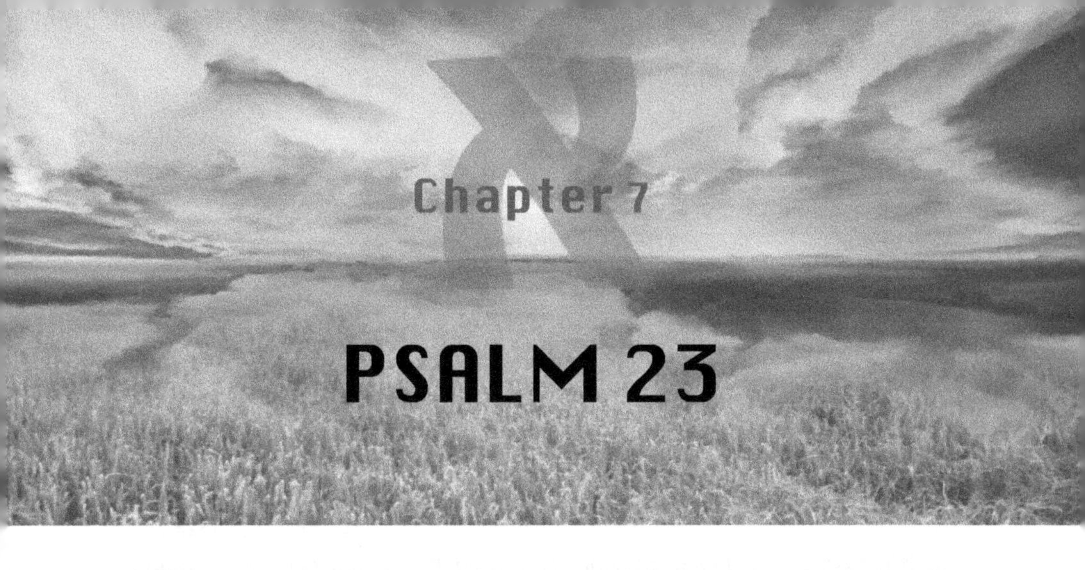

Chapter 7

PSALM 23

One of the things I emphasized at the beginning of this book is we've been brought up to think that the world is operating in lack.

Consequently, we spend our whole lives trying to protect what we think is going to run out. Ultimately, this means that we really don't believe in God, but rather we believe in ourselves. If that is the case, then we really don't know God the way we think we do. If we really knew God, we would know that He never runs out. It's very simple - you learned this in Sunday school. Society, however, tells you that everything in the world is running out. I now understand why the bible is so "anti city." The bible actually considers a city to be the presence of all kinds of evil, where human beings are brought together to be controlled and not allowed to spread themselves upon the face of the earth.

All the human beings on earth today can fit into the state of Texas when standing side-by-side. However, we are told that the earth doesn't have any more land and we believe it. We are huddled into cities and are made to step on each other and psychologically we believe as we are told. Through various forms of media, we get the message that if we don't kill the next person to us to get what we want, it is going to run out. We have actually bought into that notion. God's command to His people - Adam, Noah, and their children - was to go East, spread out across the land, and subdue it. To spread out over the earth was the command, but instead they huddled together to build a tower of confusion. We recall the first city on earth was built by Cain for his son, based on the blood of Abel whom Cain murdered.

You may not agree, but villagers in rural areas don't generally go about murdering each other. They don't have as much crime as we do in cities. Every human being on earth can have two to three acres of land and the earth will still have enough land. Recall what you see out of an airplane window. Not many areas are densely populated. I'm not a conspiracy theorist, but this is really what the Luciferians have done to humanity. They've convinced us that we cannot survive living alone somewhere in the mountain and that God is incapable of protecting us. They've convinced us that if we move away from the city we are going to die of hunger. Ironically, all the food we eat comes from outside of the city and brought into the city. This seems like common sense, but as my father says, common sense is not so common!

Common sense is not so common

I am not against cities, but I think that cities take too much upon themselves and they want to control everybody. Do you sometimes wonder why God took away Jerusalem that was on earth? When God took away Jerusalem and it became the city of the Jebusites, it became a city of blood. Don't take that as a political statement because it's not intended to be. Even the reason God destroyed the Jerusalem of Israel in the first place was because it had become a place of blood, as we are told by Jeremiah, Ezekiel, and Isaiah. It wasn't destroyed because the foreigners were strong; it was destroyed because we filled Jerusalem with blood from one end to the other. We gathered the people and we made idols and worshiped them.

Nobody actually criticizes the cities anymore. Prophets today talk as if the cities were created by God, when in fact they are human systems created for confusion and control. It is in cities that families break up easily. There are not that many prostitutes in the rural areas, are there? For those of you who think you're civilized because you live in the city, think again. The city is a place where barbarians live and hurt one another and fight over crumbs, while there is plenty outside of the city. If you were living out in the desert and you had a piece of land, you could grow your own food. In the next few years, people are actually going to live outside of cities and come into them primarily for interaction. Cities are not sustainable. Think about what they're doing now in New York City, stacking people up on top of each other. Is there not enough land in the state of New York for those people to live? I just think that we over-value city-living. This doesn't mean they don't have some good things about them, but the same things you do in the city you can do in the rural areas. You can scatter yourselves and still do what you do in cities.

Every time human beings have done what we are doing now, God has come and scattered them. Read your scripture. I don't know what the answer is, but I'm saying that we shouldn't idolize the city because it is not what it's cracked up to be. Children who were born in cities think the city is the place God wants us to be, but there are enough resources in creation and enough space on earth for all of us. I flew across Asia and saw vast lands out of the airplane window. I know there are a billion people in China, but where were they? Most of them are gathered in different cities together. In the US, you can fly across this nation and see the amazing availability of land, yet certain groups of people want to take it and make it their own so that we have to beg them for it.

So we will notice that all the things that God does is to show us that we are actually candidates and embodiments of the process of abundance.

It's a system that leads to the systematic enslavement of humanity and yet we've made it out to be such a great thing. You need to look at these worldly structures with some skepticism. I'm not saying you should leave the city and go to a rural area. Most city people would have a difficult time surviving outside of the city, but I'm saying we need to begin to think differently. There are enough resources on the face of the earth and if we mature to become who we are supposed to be in God, we can also help create more resources. On the other hand, if we focus on fighting over the little things, operating in lack, we find ourselves not living in peace. All wars are fought over resources and somebody convinces somebody else that there's not enough of it so they are ready to die to get it.

There was a time when we were led to believe that gold was running out and then all of a sudden we were being told they had discovered even more gold than ever before. We have to think from this perspective and apply it to our personal lives. Ask yourself whether you operate from the position of lack or from the position of abundance. The answer determines your psychological and spiritual well-being, David said, "I operate from the position of abundance, from the position that God is the shepherd, full of blessing, and He releases it towards me." So we will notice that all the things that God does is to show us that we are actually candidates and embodiments of the process of abundance.

Psalm 23:6 says,

"Surely goodness and mercy shall follow me all the days of my life."

Surely	אַיִי (ach)
Goodness	טוֹב (to·vv)
And mercy	וָחֶסֶד (va·che·sed)
Will follow me	יִרְדְּפוּנִי (yir·de·fu·ni)
All the days of my life	כָּל יְמֵי חַיָּי (kol yemei chayah)

When you start looking at the way that this text is structured, you'll notice that the first word is comprised of the first letters of the names of the fathers of Israel - Abraham, Isaac, and Jacob. So the word "ach" becomes **Aleph Yod Yod** which is Abraham, Yitzchak, Yaakov. Remember God said, "I am the God of Abraham" in Exodus 3:6 and He says that this will be His name forever. Jesus repeats the declaration in Matthew 22:32. In the Jewish tradition, Abraham is considered to be the carrier of mercy. Now when David says, "Surely goodness and mercy shall follow me all the days of my life," we know that he is referring to God's goodness and God's mercy, two key aspects of His nature. However, when Israelites pray, they say "the mercies of Abraham" which is considered the ever-flowing river from heaven that flows into their hearts. It's a reference to God's nature flowing through the patriarch Abraham and his seed, Isaac and Jacob. Israel is actually the recipient of mercy because God said to Abraham that He would have mercy on them and cause His goodness to pass before them. (Exodus 33:19) God does this continuously. The way this works for David is a genetic channel whereby God is constantly following him. For us, it works through the Son of God, Jesus Christ, who carries the goodness and the mercy of God.

Let's look at the gematria of a few of these words. The gematria of ach **(אַיִי)**is 21. Two plus one is three which is not only the number of God but also the number of the ancestors of Israel. So when a Jew says Abraham, Isaac, and Jacob they are actually referring to God because it is the name that God took for himself. He's the God of Abraham Isaac and Jacob.

Goodness cannot germinate where someone is not willing to die.

Tovv is the word for goodness and its gematria is eight. The funny thing about Tovv is that it begins with Tet. Tet has a numerical value of nine, which is also the number for death, Remember the story from the Zohar about when the letters to God to explain why they should be the first letter in the AlephBet? When Tet came to God and said he should be the first one because he was the beginning of Tovv. But God also became death. Now if you think about goodness, you will notice that, according to scripture, goodness flows from the capacity to die. Jesus said in John 12:24:

> "Verily, verily, I say unto you, Except a corn of wheat fall into the ground and die, it abideth alone: but if it die, it bringeth forth much fruit." (KJV)

The idea of goodness here is not about death in terms of complete demise and disappearing, but rather constant dying to oneself that allows goodness to germinate. Goodness cannot germinate where someone is not willing to die. Every act of goodness suppresses something else that is evil. In other words, every time you do something good, something in you dies that is contrary to the nature of God. This explains what Paul meant when he said, "I die daily." (1 Corinthians 15:31) Paul died by constantly doing something good. In Jewish terms, constantly doing mitzvahs demonstrates God's goodness. The usual way we operate is when we want to do something really good, there is always some doubt that comes with it. We're thinking about our own need, our own position, or what it is going to cost us. However, if we actually carry out that good act, we've killed something. We have at least begun to kill the mindset of operating from lack and out of that death , goodness germinates. I discovered that I don't need to be looking for a way to crucify myself and that doing good actually is crucifixion. If I go out and I share kindness with somebody who does not deserve it, I have actually crucified myself without having to go through the pain of actually understanding what I'm doing in the process of crucifixion.

The next word is mercy or "chesed" **(חֶסֶד)** . The first letter is Chet**(חֶ)** which has a numerical value of 8. Chet is a closed door which you cannot go into unless you are initiated. Chet, although it looks like Heh **(ה)** it is very different. Heh is a door with the hinges on it because it the Dalet **(ד)** and the Vav **(ו)** together. However, Chet is just a closed door. In the mystery realm, when you come to the door of Chet, you must die in order to cross over. It's not physical death—it is an initiation into mysteries. So Chet is the door that stands in front of someone who is not initiated. For you to be able to enter the closed door you need mercy. You can't enter unless we are prayed in mercy.

So the numerical value of Chet is eight and the gematria of the word Tovv is eight. What this means is that the only way for God's goodness to become real in your life, for you to actually understand it, is for you to be initiated into the mysteries of God. If you're not initiated in the mysteries of God, then the goodness of God in your life will just appear as something taken for granted and you won't understand that the goodness of God actually brings the mysteries of heaven into your life. In Romans 2:4, the bible says,

> Or do you despise the riches of His goodness, forbearance, and longsuffering, not knowing that the goodness of God leads you to repentance? (NKJV)

God himself is the goodness.

What is repentance? Repentance is one of the principles for initiation into the mystery of the nature of God because if you don't repent you can't go in. Thus, when David talks about being followed by goodness, he's talking about this constant opportunity for initiation into the mystery of divinity. The mystery of God has to do with the fullness of God and the fact that God never runs out of anything. The simple mystery is if you are in God, you're complete. So goodness is not just something that God *has*. ***God himself is the goodness.***

The initiation of a believer into the goodness of God is an initiation into the very nature of God Himself. Again, when you stand in front of a good act that you're supposed to do, you're standing in front of a door of the mystery of initiation. Every time you're called to do something great and good, you're standing in front of a closed door and only the act of goodness can open it. You are standing in front of an initiatory process into an aspect of divinity. God gives us opportunities to be initiated to a dimension of His being every day and every moment by bringing crazy people into our lives that we're supposed to help or by just making your family crazy enough so you can help them. He comes in all kinds of ways so that you can understand that, because of the interest of God in your life and the vastness of His divinity, He is always making space and putting a door in front of you to initiate you into a mystery of an aspect of His being.

The word that is translated *follow* is "yirdefuni" (יִרְדְּפוּנִי) and its gematria is 360. This number is a reference to going full circle. David is saying that goodness and mercy will follow me and initiate me into the mysteries of the nature of God and also the mystery of the fullness of creation. Therefore, if I operate in the fullness of who God is, if I operate in God's abundance, I'm always brought to the place of the fullness of creation. I'm brought to the full circle which is comprised of His never-ending goodness and mercy.

God's fullness never runs out

Every time I get into a position of lack, I can actually restart the principle that causes the inflow of divine plenitude into my life By going back the process of creation in Genesis 1 on the sixth day. By operating in God's abundance, I can always go full circle. It's important to know that goodness and mercy pursue me. They chase after me; I'm not chasing after them. They're not in front of me. They're behind me. They're chasing after me because fullness and abundance are overflowing principles of God. He is eager to break open the door so that I can be inundated with all that God has in store for me. The gematria of 360 tells me that this overflow is all around me all the days of my life!

You live in the world where your mindset is lack and you think God even created the earth to run out. But you can constantly come back to Him who is the fullness of everything. God sends His goodness and mercy, which is Himself, to be available at the point of your need so that every time you run out, goodness and mercy meet to create an arc to manifest the vision of what is coming from the realm of divinity into your life. In other words, you really never run out. The only place you run out is in your head. If you are a child of God, your first task when you begin to operate from lack is to turn yourself towards God, God's fullness never runs out.

The last words of "all the days of my life" is yemey khayay (יְמֵי חַיַּי). Yemey is spelled Yod Mem Yod and has a numerical value of 60, which is the number of creation. This is all about returning to the point of the creation of man and using the principles of creation to reformulate your life, to rectify your life, to reenergize your life, to re-scroll your life, and to redirect your life. The gematria of khayay is ten. Chet (8), Yod (10), Yod (10) equals 28. Two plus eight equals ten. So you begin the whole passage with three (Abraham, Isaac, and Jacob) and you end up with the principle of creation. David is saying he operates in the fullness of the promise that was made to Abraham, Isaac, and Jacob, Not only that but he operates as a person who constantly stands in the presence of the door of divine mystery. The door is closed, but I always have access because of what is behind me.

I thus have access to this door, but not everyone who comes to the door is initiated and so the door for them is closed. Anyone who doesn't know the God of these three people, who comes to this door can't access anything. It is what follows behind you that actually determines what happens to your future because remember whatever you place behind you, you will harvest in the future. Your future is being pushed towards you by that which stands behind you. Why does God make it a constant duty to forgive you? Because God doesn't want anything behind you but Himself. God doesn't want anything else chasing you but Him. David will always sin, but he does not say, "Oh my goodness! All my sins are following me! What am I going to do?" Rather, he says, "Surely, goodness and mercy are chasing me." This is not something that happens one day and then never again. David goes on to say that they will pursue him all the days of his life. In fact, they are pursuing him even into the grave. Now if goodness and mercy pursue me all the days of my life and my life truly doesn't end when I die, this means that they pursue me all the way to the next world! When believers die in this world, they don't leave to go to the dirt, they go to a new life.

There's no end to the believer's abundance.

God follows me even into the grave. On the other side of the realm, God's goodness and mercy continue to chase me because they pursue me eternally The goodness and mercy of God - demonstrated through Abraham, Isaac, and Jacob - is still alive and constantly chasing their descendants. It is truth that allows Jesus to say that God is not a God of the dead; He's the God of the living (Luke 20:38). For a believer this chasing allows them to start again. There's no end to the believer's abundance.

Remember, we are the ones who say there's an end to abundance, it is us who operate in the lack and we operate that way, we don't give because we think we don't have enough. We don't move towards meeting other people's needs because we worry about what will happen to us. It bears repeating; we don't think from the perspective of the flow of abundance. We believe we never have enough to be able to do anything for anyone else until we can provide for ourselves.

You have to understand the letter Dalet is an open door with the hinges on it. In contrast, the letter Chet is a closed Dalet. Think about how all of this relates to Jesus saying, "I am the door." (John 10:9) The book of John contains a lot of the themes from Psalm 23: I'm the Good Shepherd; I came that they might have life and have it more abundantly; I am the door; by me the Sheep go in and out and find pasture. David is telling you Psalm 23 should be the anthem of the believer.

God is constantly removing that which is a hindrance between you and Him by the blood of his Son to make sure that you have constant access to the fullness of your Father in heaven.

When I first became a Christian, every church I went to would recite two prayers: "Our 'Father who art in heaven" and "the Lord is my shepherd." Until the Lord told me to teach Psalm 23, I didn't realize that it should be our mantra. God is the embodiment of over abundance, overflowing abundance, hyper abundance, and supernatural abundance! He tells us,

I carry this and I pursue you with it. When you put a block between me and you, I use the blood of my Son to take it away so that you can always have access. No, so ***I*** can always have access to pour it upon you. I want to bless you. I want to fill you with my goodness. I do not have a problem, you do. Surely goodness and mercy shall follow you all the days of your life. It includes both the days of your earthly existence as well as the days of your eternity!

This is about you as someone who knows God operating in your life the way Adam operated in the garden. God's intention for you as his child is to bring you constantly to the position of the full supply that Adam had in the garden where there was no sin and no lack. This is the reason for being born from above and becoming a child of God. If your sin is a problem, then Jesus died in vain because all you need to do is go to Him, to his blood. God is constantly removing that which is a hindrance between you and Him by the blood of his Son to make sure that you have constant access to the fullness of your Father in heaven. There's nothing between you and God that's holding you back right now. Get ready for an incredible life operating from the place of the full supply of the father's heart for you! God continues to pursue you to manifest the fullness of who He is. Amen.

Jesus tells us He is the door, the good shepherd who feeds the sheep and the lambs. He tells us that He came that we might have life and have it more abundantly and that He is the door we can go in and out of and find pasture. If your reason for God not blessing you is because of your shortcomings, for what reason is He blessing the unbeliever? You need to get away from that kind of thinking. This doesn't mean you shouldn't walk righteously. It means that this is not a reason why God blesses you. God blesses you because He's God and because you believe that He will bless you. The bible doesn't say with sin or without sin it is impossible to please God. It says "Without faith, it's impossible to please God." (Hebrews 11:6) There is a reason God put that faith there. It is by faith you are forgiven. It is by faith you are healed. It is by faith that you access God. That faith is the person of Christ. He is that door you can't run away from. You can operate in abundance if you understand this every time you do something good. Remember, you are opening a door of mystery. Every time you believe God you're opening a door, but the door follows you everywhere. You don't have to seek for the door - it pursues you. It follows you. It's the door of goodness and mercy! Amen.

God blesses you because He's God and because you believe that He will bless you.

Appendix A: The Hebrew Aleph Bet

Letter	Name	Numerical Value
א	Aleph	1
ב	Bet	2
ג	Gimel	3
ד	Dalet	4
ה	Heh	5
ו	Vav	6
ז	Zayin	7
ח	Chet	8
ט	Tet	9
י	Yod	10
כ	Kaph	20
ל	Lamed	30
מ	Mem	40
נ	Nun	50
ס	Samech	60
ע	Ayin	70
פ	Pay	80
צ	Tsade	90
ק	Qoph	100
ר	Resh	200
ש	Shin	300
ת	Tav	400

ABOUT THE AUTHOR

Adonijah Okechukwu Ogbonnaya (BA, MATS, MA, Ph.D) is the founder of AACTEV8 International, an Apostolic and Kingdom Ministry which works with the Body of Christ across the globe for Soul Winning, Discipleship, Training, and Equipping the saints in Kingdom mysteries and Kingdom living. Located in Venice, California, Dr. Ogbonnaya (also known as A. Okechukwu or "Dr. O") began preaching the Word of God in the 1970s in his teenage years. He has served as a missionary, church planter, pastor, and professor. Dr. Ogbonnaya has traveled and ministered in over 25 nations in Asia, Africa, Europe, and North and South America with the message of the Gospel of Jesus Christ. He has seen God perform various signs and wonders as He promised in Mark 16:1–17—the blind receive sight, the deaf hear, the lame walk, the dead are raised, the barren receive the fruit of the womb, lives are transformed and minds renewed. He has focused on helping believers engage the spiritual realities which have been opened up for them in the person of the Lord Jesus Christ. He is a Hebrew-born native of Nigeria, West Africa. He earned his Ph.D and Master's degree in theology and personality and his Master's in religion from Claremont School of Theology. He completed his M.A. in theological studies at Western Evangelical Seminary and his B.A. in religion at Hillcrest Christian College in Canada. He also holds a Ph.D in business publishing.

He is also the presenter of numerous teachings found at: www.aactev8.com.

Dr. Ogbonnaya is married to Pastor Benedicta and is blessed with four wonderful children and grandchildren.

Seraph Creative is a collective of artists, writers, theologians & illustrators who desire to see the body of Christ grow into full maturity, walking in their inheritance as Sons Of God on the Earth.

Sign up to our newsletter to know about the release of the next book in the series, as well as other exciting releases.

Visit our website :
www.seraphcreative.org

אתה

Lightning Source UK Ltd.
Milton Keynes UK
UKHW021823060223
416559UK00012B/2270